From Meth to Manhood to Ministry

By: Bobby Shane Brooks

The Christian Writer's Workshop
World Changers Bible School
Year 1 Quarter 4

Word Count: 13,933
Page Count: 46
Date: February 20, 2016

Bobby Shane Brooks

Religion / Biblical Studies

Book Cover Design by Bobby Shane Brooks

Special thanks to editors Wanda E. Hudson and Robyn L. Norwood

For worldwide distribution, Printed in the USA

ISBN-13:978-1530374243-
ISBN-10:150374243

Bobby Shane Brooks

<u>Dedication</u>

To my wife, my children and my parents who never seem to give up on me.

Bobby Shane Brooks

CONTENTS

PREFACE/FORWARD
INTRODUCTION

Chapter 1   **Me**   6

Chapter 2   **Meth**   8

Chapter 3   **Mess**   13

Chapter 4   **More Mess**   20

Chapter 5   **Manhood**   25

Chapter 6   **Ministry**   30

Call to Salvation   44
About the Author

Bobby Shane Brooks

INTRODUCTION

I am told there are 129 million different book titles to read both online and in print, and you are reading this one, thank you! As I begin this book I think about the people that may be reading it and what it is that we all have in common. We all want to be free. Bondage doesn't only come as an addiction to a substance. Some people are in bondage to substances. Some people are in bondage to pornography. Some are in bondage to bad thinking. Any type of bondage that you have experienced is a trick from the enemy to keep you from reaching the final destination God has chosen for your life. No matter how the devil has been attacking you, my prayer is that as you read this book, you begin to understand your identity in Christ. I pray that the chains that have been keeping you bound (bondage) begin to fall off.

As an author I'm thankful anyone would take the time to read something I would write, but more than that I pray this book be a tool utilized to set people free. This is not a self-help book, but a Christ help book.

Bobby Shane Brooks

Now, I caution you; as we journey forward into this book sometimes it may seem quite graphic, but in order for me to give testimonial and demonstrate how good life has become for me, I must give an account of how bad it was as well. So tighten up your boot straps and let's begin this journey!

Isaiah 49:9 to say to the captives 'Come out' and to those in darkness 'Be Free!'

Bobby Shane Brooks

CHAPTER 1

ME

Using Methamphetamine did much more than grant the ability to stay awake for days and weeks at a time; it was actually my painkiller. The physical and emotional pain I experienced ceased whenever I was high. Let me explain how this all began.

When I was in fifth grade my parents divorced. They were never taught the importance of a covenant relationship nor how it may affect children. This was the beginning of extremely rebellious behavior from me and my brother Chris. At first we stayed with our mom, but with all the new changes happening in our lives we rebelled even more. Eventually, my mother remarried so "we" decided "we" would go live with our dad.

Now, before I go any further let me state clearly that I love my dad. He is my champion and a wonderful grandfather to my children, but during those days he was more of a brother than a dad.

Bobby Shane Brooks

He had no more of an idea of who he was or his identity than we, as kids, did. No matter how many girlfriends my brother and I had, my dad always seemed to be interested in their mothers, as most of our girlfriends came from divorced families as well. I can remember hanging out with my dad at age sixteen. I remember our girlfriends and how I used a fake ID to get into a club in Atlanta called the Crystal Palace. This club would remain a large part of my life as I built my testimony, so there is more to come about "the Palace". Anyway, drug use, being anything from alcohol to amphetamine was an acceptable activity during my high school years. Without anyone to really stop me, my drug use became more and more of a daily activity. Needless to say, both my grades and relationships began to suffer. My then girlfriend was definitely uninterested in continuing a monogamous relationship with a practicing drug addict. She was smart enough to realize this wasn't something she wanted contribute to her future. So the inevitable happened. When I discovered that she had been with someone else, I experienced a pain unlike any pain I had ever felt. I had to make it stop! I continued to use so the pain

Bobby Shane Brooks

would subside, but it was a temporary fix felt only during the high. This cycle fueled the addiction and it became full-fledged.

As I look back, getting over a girlfriend without using drugs would have been simpler than allowing this heartbreak to become a catalyst for an 18 year drug addiction!

Just an interesting side note; the number 18 represents bondage in the Word of God. An example of this was the daughter of Abraham, bound 18 years in Luke 13:16. There were also 18 sinners, or people, who were in bondage to sin in Luke 13:4-5. Maybe one more? Ok, on two different occasions in the book of Judges, the children of Israel were found in bondage to their enemies 18 years. Judges 3:14 - 10:7-8. Don't you find the Word extremely interesting!

Ok, back to the subject at hand. The use of drugs such as alcohol and marijuana are a gateway to more dangerous and addictive drugs. This is what the devil will do; plant a seed and reap a later harvest. My amphetamine use eventually became intravenous and what a slippery slope! This method of introduction is so vastly different than snorting, swallowing or smoking drugs. I would like to

Bobby Shane Brooks

focus on this chapter in my life in the next chapter of this book, as I believe my willingness to try IV methods both accelerated and deepened the addiction.

Bobby Shane Brooks

CHAPTER 2

METH

As I begin writing the second chapter, I just want to express my love towards God. I want to thank Him for being patient with me and for never giving up on me. If you are reading my book I want you to know that God has never and will never give up on you! Hebrews chapter 13 says that He will never leave us and never forsake. Romans 8:1 clearly states that there is no condemnation for those of us who are in Christ Jesus. Right now someone may be thinking "how is that legal" (possible, allowable)? How is it that He would never leave me nor forsake me with all the sin I've experienced in my life? The reason why it is completely legal for God to never leave us nor forsake us, even in the middle of our sin, is because He already forsook His Son on the cross!

As you read details in this chapter of how bad this experience was for me, I want you to think about how much God loves you. He loves you so much that He sent His very own Son to trade places with you (John 3:16 For God so loved the world, that He gave His only begotten Son, that whosoever believeth in Him should not perish, but have everlasting life). He forsook Jesus so that He would never have to forsake us. Jesus went to hell so that you and I would never have to go! Know that He loves you.

Without an enabler, very few drug addicts are able to take the addiction as far as I did. An enabler is someone who enables another to persist in self-destructive behavior by providing excuses or by making it possible to avoid the consequences. For me, that was my grandmother. Just like most enablers, she had no idea the love she thought she was expressing towards me was actually enabling me to dig further and further into the addiction. Let me explain. When I first became a drug addict, my focus was merely using more and more drugs. I didn't have to focus on "how" I could get those drugs. I lived with my grandmother when I left high school. Having a place to stay, provided by her, allowed me to spend whatever money I had on drugs. Saying "no" and demonstrating tough love were two disciplines my grandmother knew nothing about. Most drug addicts I have met in life seemed to do the same thing which is exhaust any family member's ability to enable. If there lies no ability within a drug addict's persona to hustle and make things happen, I am of the persuasion that the addiction, being poorly funded, would come to a conclusion much quicker. Sometimes tough love and saying "no" is the best love there is!

I graduated high school in 1987, but continued to live with my grandmother. In 1989, I was introduced to another method of getting high: using a needle. I was working at a mill in Griffin called Dundee Towels. The part that I worked in was called the bleachery. This was where the towels were bleached, stretched and dyed. One night, as I was working, I jumped off a towel pit. I wore a sheath on my side, and the scissors in the sheath had worn a whole in the bottom of the sheath. When I landed the bottom of the scissors opened up the skin around the inside of my wrist (the scar from this injury is still on my right wrist).Of course management sent me to Spalding Hospital to receive treatment and get the wound sewed up. At the hospital (of all places) my life forever changed. The doctor

Bobby Shane Brooks

who sewed me up noticed that I was high on some type of stimulant: I guess eyes as big as the bottom of a coke bottle is some type of clue! I will never forget this; we were the only two in the emergency room that they put me in, and as he sewed me up he asked what kind of drugs I was using. I told him I was high on cocaine. Then this doctor, a man who had taken an oath "to do no harm", asked if he could buy some cocaine from me! Of course I thought that he was setting me up considering I was so high, but he assured me he also used cocaine and that he only wanted to see how good mine was. A couple of days later he called me and I went to his house. This was my first experience seeing someone use drugs intravenously. I am actually thankful I learned to shoot drugs from someone in the medical field because he taught me to never ever share a needle. Throughout my entire drug use I never shared a needle. The way this guy used drugs literally blew my mind. When I sold him 1/2 ounce of cocaine, he placed a butterfly in his arm and used the same hole to shoot his drugs. The next night I went back to his house to find him in his backyard, halfway up a tree, completely naked. He informed me that he was doing "recon". CRAZY! Why that would appeal to

Bobby Shane Brooks

me, I have no idea, but that second night I used drugs for the first time intravenously. He taught me things that only someone in the medical field would know, like how to use shadows to find a vein and how to only use a needle once because after it broke the skin it would only be half as sharp. Most drug addicts, who use drugs intravenously, share needles and use them over and over again. This was something I never did. One of the silly mottos I had during my drug use was "if you're going to be stupid at least be smart about being stupid". He told me that he never used while practicing medicine, but that he would take time off so that he could use drugs. The way a drug addict will justify his drug use is still a mystery to me.

Cocaine, for me, was never really what caused such a lengthy drug addiction. What I did was very similar to a heroin addict becoming addicted to methadone. Once I used methamphetamine intravenously, I never used cocaine again. Cocaine was extremely potent, but coming off of it or running out of it was almost painful. I reached a point where going up was not really worth coming down.

Bobby Shane Brooks

The thing about methamphetamine is you never really come down. I think the longest period for me to go without sleep was 17 days! But eventually you do fall asleep. For most addicts, once awake they would, of course, use the bathroom, get something to eat, then go back to bed. Not me. The first thing I would reach for would be the dope. As I look back on my behavior I believe I was one of the worst methamphetamine addicts to ever walk the earth. Picture someone without clothes in a hotel room, sitting in a lawn chair, with Halogen construction lights surrounding them just for the purpose of finding a vein…that was my life with meth! There was a time I was extremely ashamed of my behavior but now, being aware of my identity in Christ, I am just thankful I'm still alive!

People have often asked me, "why do you think the addiction lasted as long as it did?"
I really think I stayed as high as I did because of the condemnation I learned at church. When I was a kid my mother took me to a church in Riverdale Georgia called Riverdale Assembly of God. This church taught me I was saved by what Jesus did on the cross, but that I

Bobby Shane Brooks

would only maintain my salvation by my behavior and what I did in life: by my good works. I knew methamphetamine use had caused me to "lose" my salvation. Because I thought I had lost my salvation, in my mind, the condemnation could only be remedied with more drug use. I really thought this "Jesus guy" was impossible to work for. Never forget that any time you're accused by the *(accuser)* himself, it never lines up with your true identity. The salvation I have now is the same salvation I had then, and it has never been based on my behavior, but on what Jesus had already done; His obedience to our heavenly Father!

If you have made it this far reading this book, don't put it down now. I'm aware the foundation I am laying involves much graphic details about drug use, but let's face it, are there any details about drug use that are not graphic? In this next chapter I will focus on the creativity I used to buy drugs. This creativity enabled me to experience a lifestyle that really was from the pit of hell. If you are thinking now that you would like to put this book down, I urge you to give it just one more chapter.

Bobby Shane Brooks

CHAPTER 3

MESS

If you are reading this I literally want you to take out your identification whether it be a driver's license, military ID or whatever you use as identification and hold it in your hand. Now, I want you to take your keys and hold them in your other hand. As you hold your ID in one hand, and your keys in the other I want you to know that the "*key*" to the entire Christian walk is knowing who you are! As you read this chapter you will realize I never knew my identity in Christ. I also never knew my actual value was equivalent to the price Jesus paid for me! No one ever told me I was loved by God and that the price that was paid for me on the cross was actually a revelation of how much He loves Bobby Shane Brooks. I want you to know that He loves you so much He was willing to embrace sin (filthy humanity) and allow the hands of His own creation to put Him to death! He paid such a price BECAUSE He loves you that much

(John 3:16)! In order for you to begin to understand your TRUE identity I want you to think about one scripture as you read this third chapter: 1 John 4:17, in the King James version, this phenomenal scripture reads," Herein is our love made perfect, that we may have boldness in the day of judgement: because as He is, so are we in this world." So think about it this way, is Jesus sick? NO!! Is Jesus broke? NO!! Is Jesus a drug addict receiving His identity from a behavior? EMPHATICALLY NO!! Then neither are you....because as He is so are we! (Praise God!)

Once I began to identify myself the way the world did because of my actions and behavior, I began to embrace the lifestyle of daily drug use. Drug use comes with figuring out some kind of way to do drugs daily! Drugs are expensive and this is why so much crime surrounds drug use. My story is not an exception to this rule. The concept of pay to play must have originated here. My next chapter will discuss some of the consequences of meth use, but I want to share some of the really inventive and clever ways I funded an eighteen year addiction to methamphetamine.

Bobby Shane Brooks

One silly motto I had was "Nothing exceeds like excess!" To have an excessive amount of methamphetamine cost an excessive amount of money. Most people believe that all drug addicts sell drugs, and this is true to some extent, but my problem was mathematical. I would sell one ounce of dope, but I used two ounces! "Don't get high on your own supply" was not a motto that I subscribed to, so I had to use my brain to fund this crazy lifestyle.

It is true that incarceration is like a training ground for criminal activity. It was during repetitive past incarcerations that my eyes were opened to the many tricks and schemes I could do on the outside in order to live this "meth addicted lifestyle". One of these "bright ideas" came about when I witnessed how inmates would steal food. They would actually get in line twice! They would sit the first tray of food they received on the table and get in line again to receive a second tray (no accountability). This behavior made me think about how big box stores, such as Home Depot and Lowe's, never had anyone standing at the door to check receipts. In my mind anyone could simply get an item and walk right out with it. The

Bobby Shane Brooks

problem with this method of shoplifting was that most items have an internal tag that would trigger a sensor at the door. These alarms make a lot of noise and any meth user will tell you that the last thing you want to do is make noise!! So I realized this was not such a good idea because even though a person could usually get away (especially if they had a car waiting like they were doing a bank robbery), making that kind of noise was not for me. Around this time, copper and aluminum prices were also really high, so I was constantly on the lookout for any spools of wire at job sites or around warehouses; not really what you would call living in prosperity! The problem: when using a roll of wire, the plastic around the copper has to be melted or stripped off. This was not my idea of a way to make a lot of money: looking for scrap metal was not going to fund the habit I had developed. What would?

One day while in Home Depot I noticed a spool of speaker wire called monster cable, which sold for $0.99 a foot or $485.00 for the entire 500 foot roll. Because this item was sold by the foot and very rarely by the spool, it did not have a sensor that would set off

Bobby Shane Brooks

the alarms at the door. I concluded the snatch would be simple. I would put the speaker wire in a buggy and roll it to the front of the store, then I would put the spool on my shoulder and simply walk out. Brilliant right? The only problem is, (and you knew there would be one ~ since a meth addict is only brilliant in his own mind), there's not a lot of black market requests for speaker wire!

After this, I came up with what I thought was another brilliant scheme. Because their computers only held six months of recording transactions, I would call Home Depot and ask to speak to a manager. Once I got a manger on the phone my story went like this: "my grandfather died about six months earlier and his will is being disputed by my aunt. Now that the courts have indeed given the property involved in the will to my grandmother, she wants me to finish a project my grandfather started. The project consists of property that my grandparents own called Opry House. Immediately before he died, my grandfather was in the process of building a quality sound system for a nightclub where older generations would come on the weekend to listen to bluegrass music. Unfortunately, my grandfather bought the wrong size speaker wire and bought way too much of it. I only needed 200 feet of speaker wire not 500 to finish wiring the Opry House. Needless to say after all this time I cannot produce a receipt." *Just an interesting side note, my grandmother did go to the Hollonville Opry House on the weekends and her favorite band was called the Orange Possum Special!*

Now, Home Depot had these 50 foot spools of speaker wire that were $22 a piece. What the manager would do is take back the speaker wire "that my grandfather bought", exchange it for four 50-foot spools of the next smaller size speaker wire, totaling $88 for $22 a spool, give me a receipt for the four spools of 50-foot wire, then give the $412 balance back in cash. I would then go to another Home Depot and get the $88 back. It took some time, but generally in just a few hours I would have $518.36 and would do this scam sometimes twice a day. I can talk freely about this because the statute of limitations has long run out. I literally did this all over the southeast. I even kept logs and journals about the different managers at the different Home Depot's that I would frequent trying my best not to say the same story to the same manager. After a while I even began doing this at Lowe's.

Sometimes instead of doing the same scam I would do something a little different. I would go into a store with just a few hundred dollars. I would then find an item that had a price tag of at least $600. Pressure washers and generators were great for this because I could get $.50 on the dollar for anything brand new from my "fence", who just so happened to be my meth dealer. I would take a pressure washer that was $300 and another pressure washer priced at $600, put them both in my buggy, then head straight to returns. I would tell the folks in customer service that I bought the smaller version, but didn't have a receipt and was interested in buying the more expensive item and I would pay the difference in cash. Most shoplifters are flat broke and contemplate a get away with whatever they can stuff down their pants. Because cash money was involved to pay the difference in this scam, I was highly successful in leaving with a $600 item with only $300 invested. My problem: considering all my fence would give me is $.50 on the

Bobby Shane Brooks

dollar, I would only get $300. No problem though right? I mean they had given me a $600 receipt for a $600 item and I could return for the entire $600, right? Not so fast! You see any time a return was fashioned in this manner, because an original receipt was not produced for the smaller priced item, Home Depot and Lowe's would write ATP on the receipt in big bold letters as a way to stop professional shoplifters like myself. *I bet this method was usually highly successful, but not when it came to dealing with Bobby Shane.* ATP stood for "apply to purchase" which meant this receipt, no matter the value, could only be used to apply to another purchase, no cash back! Wow, all that work and now I had a $600 item with a $600 receipt and all I could do is get an in store credit! Let me tell you how I fixed this problem. I would simply write a K before the ATP, change the P to an R then write INA after. Now instead of it saying ATP it said KATRINA. Then I would put a made up phone number like (770) 787-0812 underneath. *(If this book becomes a great best seller and this is your phone number, please forgive me, truly random!)* I would tell the people at the return counter that I had used the receipt as a scrap piece of paper to write down a phone number and I would physically rewrite the number on another blank piece of paper right in front of them to absolutely convince them this receipt was legitimate. Problem solved! Now the receipts had barcodes on them and I think I am actually responsible for both big box stores making the change so that this type of criminal activity is no longer possible. As a matter of fact neither store carry the speaker wire that really fueled my behavior for literally 10+ years.

I imagine at one point my patience was running too thin to take all day running these scams, so I came up with another way to remove merchandise from Home Depot. This was probably the gutsiest way of all the shoplifting that I'd done did but it was super simple.

One day in the Home Depot I saw an orange apron lying beside a counter. I grabbed it and left the store. Returning to the store with the apron on, I put my own name on it where it says "Hello my name is (blank) How can I help you?" I would help out a customer if asked, then get on a forklift and drive out the front door with a Generac generator that cost $3,500 and simply load it onto my truck bed. I would then just leave the forklift in the parking lot.

Eventually I became quite uneasy about doing these criminal activities, so I came up with what I thought was a solution to my problem (another brilliant idea). One day while sitting in a hotel room I decided to call the home offices of both Home Depot, which is in Atlanta, and the Lowe's Corporation located in Wilmington North Carolina. I asked to speak to the loss prevention department and told them I was taking around $100,000 a year out of their stores. I told them I would stop if each company would pay me $400 cash a week. To make the deal more appealing I actually told them that I would meet them at any store of their choosing at a moment's notice to demonstrate that their security and loss prevention techniques were insufficient! I was so out of my mind I wanted the people I was shoplifting from to pay me to quit and become a consultant! How crazy is that?

Bobby Shane Brooks

Right now I'm certain you are thinking, this guy must have been out of his mind. I want to go ahead and confess to you that you are exactly right. What I want you to realize is that if you are born again, you have the mind of Christ! Romans 8:6 says, "For to be carnally minded is death; but to be spiritually minded is life and peace." That is what my life demonstrated at this point, DEATH. 1 Corinthians 2:16 emphatically states that we have the mind of Christ! The mind of the Anointed One and His anointing dwells on the inside of us! It was an actual case of mistaken identity with me. I was born again, but had no idea who I was. Remember the "key" to this whole Christian walk is knowing who you are!

I am literally embarrassed of my behavior as I read over this chapter. I don't know how this lifestyle choice would have ended had I continued single-handedly, but fortunately for me I had a little help from the criminal justice system. In my next chapter I will discuss how I was put into a position where I could actually catch my breath, clear my head of any trace of meth and, most importantly, begin to discover my true identity. Remember your identity is not found in your behavior as you are not primarily a physical body. You are a spirit and if your spirit has had a born again experience you have the very DNA of God himself!

Bobby Shane Brooks

CHAPTER 4

MORE MESS

The previous chapter was about funding a lifestyle of methamphetamine abuse. I was going to move from that directly into the consequences of behaving in such a way. However, after letting some of my family read the chapter they wanted to know, "what about this story", and "what about that story". Therefore, if you are reading this book and you're about to put it down because you've grown weary hearing about my escapades, my advice to you…skip ahead to next chapter now. However, if you have found these last chapters interesting you will be sitting on the edge of your seat by the time this one's done.

This next story will describe how I made $44,000 **in one day**. I know most would find that very hard to believe unless they worked on Wall Street, however, I truly made it by working on "the street". At the beginning of this day I was literally broke with no money in my pockets. I was with some friends and we were at a dock on Lake

Lanier. While my friends were out swimming I decided to check around me to see if there was change left in the cars; I didn't break into the cars I simply opened up the doors that were unlocked. I must have entered 8 to 10 cars and collected about $30 in change. Most of the time, during my methamphetamine use, I did not have a permanent place to live. This day was no exception. So when my friends were done swimming, I asked them to take me and my $30 to a hotel room so I could shower, use the phone, and maybe score some dope on the front (when you get something on the front you owe for it later.) The hotel was truly a $30 a night hotel. When night fell, I stepped outside to see what was going on. Next-door to the hotel was some kind of wrecker or salvage yard. When I hopped the fence to look around I noticed a window that I could enter to get inside. Burglaries and breaking and entering to a home or business was not something I did on a regular basis, but drug addiction, just like hunger, will drive a person to do very strange things. Once inside, I located a safe in the floor. Most safes are very difficult to get into without a combination and this one was no exception. I found and used a pry bar to break it open. Five hours later I was in.

Bobby Shane Brooks

What a treasure I found inside! I thought I had hit the jackpot when I discovered $18,700 in cash. What was more interesting than the money though, were the other items I found. The safe also contained five titles, which described the five brand new rollbacks that were right outside. JACK-POT! So I called a friend who dealt in stolen cars. He told me he would give me $5,000 for each roll back "I had". I took the keys which were also located in the safe along with the titles and placed the correct title and key in each vehicle. An hour later my friend showed up with four other people, paid me $25,000 in cash, and drove the rollbacks off the lot. I even opened up the gate for him and closed it back! I'm aware this story sounds so far out, but I want you to understand I was just being courageous, foolish, desperate, and extremely fortunate. You would think a methamphetamine addict with almost $44,000 in his pocket would be set for a while I really can't remember how long it was before I was broke again, but I'm sure it wasn't long.

I will also tell you about this time I used a fishing line and treble hook to fish a deposit out of a Bank of America night deposit

Bobby Shane Brooks

box. The deposit from a Hess gas station had $17,000 in cash and several thousand dollars in checks in its deposit bag. I discarded the checks, took the cash and took a limousine to Daytona Beach Florida. When I got there I got a hotel room, got out the phonebook and called three escorts to my room just so they could do my laundry! Being high on methamphetamine will ignite irrational decisions. It was literally two weeks before I had to call my mom for bus fare back home! $17,000 spent in less than two weeks on drugs... Unexplainable, unimaginable, unbelievable!

Doing drugs is not a lifestyle of glamour. I know the media and some movies portray the lifestyle as one that anybody would like to be involved in, but I'm here to tell you there's nothing glamorous about it. The last story I will share shows how ugly the lifestyle is. I was with a lady friend of mine and she wanted to go to "the bluff "in Atlanta to score some heroin. Now, for anyone reading this book who isn't a native of Atlanta and doesn't know what the "bluff " is let me explain. There are several areas in Atlanta that are known for scoring all kinds of drugs. From the bluff, to Poole Creek to Cabbagetown, dope has always been easy to get in Atlanta. This particular evening I accompanied this "friend" as she went inside of a dope trap. Now I did not use heroin, even though I tried it, but if the dope didn't rhyme (weed & speed) it wasn't for me. So I go upstairs with my friend to buy these drugs. There was a bed up there and all four posts of the bed were in buckets of kerosene! To me this was the strangest sight. I could smell the fuels, but I knew better than to ask residents any questions (I have also learned that you do not ask a woman when she is due just because she has a big stomach). I waited until we left and as soon as my friend and I got into my car I asked, "What was the bed in buckets of kerosene for?" I will never forget the look on her face as she looked at me as if I should know why. She said, "to keep the roaches off the bed, silly." WOW! Doesn't sound too glamorous does it?

I know it may be super strange to believe that someone born again would act this way. My problem was that I had no idea who I was in Christ! Being born again was just fire insurance to me. Because of *my* actions I thought there was no way I could still be

Bobby Shane Brooks

saved. I based my identity on my own behavior instead of on the finished works of Jesus and because *my* behavior was so bad I didn't see the use in even trying to change. I was convinced that the "saved" status I once had as a kid had expired due to *my* behavior. Now I have deep appreciation of how God and His grace (the unmerited, unearned, and undeserved favor of God) has changed me. Even though my spirit was recreated when I accepted Jesus early in life, my behavior lined up with my falsely perceived identity because I never allowed myself to be transformed by the renewing of my mind. Romans 12:1-2 says, "*I beseech you therefore, brethren, by the mercies of God, that ye present your bodies a living sacrifice, holy, acceptable unto God, which is your reasonable service. And be not conformed to this world: but be ye transformed by the renewing of your mind, that ye may prove what is that good, and acceptable, and perfect, will of God.*" Right believing precedes right living. If you believe right you will live right. In these last few chapters I demonstrated how I lived before my identity was discovered. Before discovering my identity, my life was doomed to failure. In fact according to Romans 6:17, my life was in reality a "servant" to

Bobby Shane Brooks

sin...*"But God be thanked, that ye were the servants of sin, but ye have obeyed from the heart that form of doctrine which was delivered you."* Paul uses the Greek word doulos which is one of the most miserable terms for a slave in the Ancient Greek language. This word describes a servant who was sold into slavery to the point that he had no destiny of his own. The slave's only responsibility was to do whatever his master wanted. His master's urges, impulses and desires were the responsibility of the slaves for the rest of the slaves life. To put it plainly, the word doulos describes one whose only existence is to fulfill the wishes or commands of his master; one whose will is completely caught up in the will of someone else. This word describes my life before I was aware of my identity. Prior to gaining knowledge of who I am in Christ I was committed to exercising my false identity. I actually thought the decisions I made were my own but, I was actually caught in the grip of sin. I didn't have a sin nature; that was removed when I was born again. But the residue from my old man was never brought under submission to my spirit man because I never fed on the Word of God. I never began the ongoing renewing of my mind. Oblivious to my identity, my

Bobby Shane Brooks

destiny was being dominated by erroneous believing. The nature I have now is the divine nature. 2 Peter 1:3-4 says, *"According as his divine power hath given unto us all things that pertain unto life and godliness, through the knowledge of him that hath called us to glory and virtue: Whereby are given unto us exceeding great and precious promises: that by these ye might be partakers of the divine nature, having escaped the corruption that is in the world through lust."* I have the DNA of God!

Ok let's move on and see what all this crazy living cost me. Indeed Jesus paid the price, in full, for all sin at the cross, but consequences still must be dealt with and paid for!

Bobby Shane Brooks

CHAPTER 5

MANHOOD

Jesus paid the eternal penalty for sin. In 1 John 2:2 the Word says He died for the sins of the entire world. I thank Him for paying such a price for me, but sometimes the consequence of sin still must be paid in the natural. This time the payer would be me. I am actually thankful I was finally held accountable to paying the price to society for my garbage. While paying for my sins, with time, I was placed in a position that allowed me to finally realize my identity. There I gained revelation of the fact that sin does not have dominion over me. I was not under the law but under grace (Romans 6:14)! It is the unmerited, unearned, and undeserved favor of God that puts you into position for sin to decrease not increase! Before writing further I just want to thank You, Jesus for shedding your blood for me so that I can be free from any dominion of sin, sickness, demons or fear! Thank You, Sir!

Bobby Shane Brooks

The first time I was arrested was at age seventeen. At that time I was finishing my junior year in high school. I was in the parking lot of the Omni Hotel in Atlanta, about to enter for a Van Halen concert. My friend and I went to Poole Creek and bought two $20 sacks of powdered cocaine. We were using a cassette tape cover to line up the drugs to snort when suddenly the police walked up to my friend's truck and opened the door. My friend was sixteen and his parents were called to come and get him, but not me, I was taken to the Atlanta Pretrial Detention Center and booked! If you are a parent reading this I really want you to comprehend what I am about to say. Don't ever prophecy over your children regarding anything about them going to jail. When we were growing up, my dad told my brother and I that he would only get us out of jail one time. By saying something of this nature you are unintentionally opening the door for your children to go to jail! Instead, decree and declare that your children will never see the inside of a jail, a prison or HELL for that matter. Proverbs **18:21** states that, *"the power of life and death is in the tongue"*. Watch carefully what you say especially over your children, your marriage, your health and your business! Proverbs

Bobby Shane Brooks

11:21 says that, " *the seed of the righteous shall be delivered*".

Declare that over your children no matter what they are doing or what it looks like in the natural. Someone reading this may believe they could never confess this scripture because they are not righteous. If you are born again YOU ARE RIGHTEOUS! Your righteousness is not based on your behavior. It is based on Jesus! Accepting what He did at Calvary far exceeds what is needed to declare you righteous. Put in your mouth what God has to say not what your flesh has to say about your life. It does not matter what it looks like. As Christians we walk by faith and not by sight (2 Corinthians 5:7)!

My dad was (and still is) a man of his word. He bonded me out of jail even though I would return again and again. This was the only time that he bonded me out. I received two years of probation and a one thousand dollar fine for Violation of the Georgia Controlled Substance Act (V.G.C.S.A) which is a felony. I also had a set of brass knuckles on me. Was I looking for trouble or what? I

Bobby Shane Brooks

wasn't even old enough to vote and I'd forfeited my right to vote. What a way to begin my adulthood!

I graduated from Morrow High School in 1987. On my senior trip to Florida I was arrested for my second felony, solicitation to the sale of cocaine. There were around eight of us in a motel room buying drugs from a guy we knew from home. There was also an undercover Bay County detective in the room buying (or rather pretending to buy!) from the same guy. I'll never forget the knock at the door. Someone looked out the window and said," It is someone with patent leather dress shoes on". Now who wears that type shoe on the beach in June except the police? This guy opened the door and I was on my way to jail for the second time with a second drug related felony. I had graduated only five days earlier! Later that year I went back to Florida to do sixty days in the Bay county jail. I used drugs for the first time at age sixteen and by my second arrest I was only eighteen with two felonies.

Bobby Shane Brooks

In 1996 I went to prison for the first time. State prison is much different from incarceration in a county lockup. Due to my age and the non-violent nature of my crimes and criminal history, I was sentenced to five years, but only had to serve one. I was given the privilege of serving the time in a boot camp. On Christmas Eve, I was released after serving only 90 days. That day I was picked up by my dad. I just couldn't wait to go get high. Going to prison does not give you a correct identity. If anything I had a new false ID..."convict!" In 1998 I violated the probation and therefore dealt a two year sentence. I was made to do this in the county jail two-for-one (sentenced to two years, yet only required to serve one). I spent an entire year in cell A-33 at the Robert A. Deyton detention facility in Lovejoy, Georgia. The same judge that sentenced me in 1996 sentenced me again in 1998. Her name is Ms. Deborah Benefield. I will be forever grateful because our relationship did not end in 1998. By 2003 I had three outstanding warrants for my arrest. What proved worse was that my girlfriend Jill, who would become my wife on September 4, 2010 was pregnant and wanted by the law for something I put her up to do. The law finally caught up to me on

Bobby Shane Brooks

July 29, 2003 while Jill was 9 months pregnant and living with her family in Alabama. What a mess!

Now I stand before Judge Benefield who sentences me to serve two years. Here is where the "Manhood" part of the book comes in. I was not there when Jill gave birth to our first child, Leviticus Shane Brooks. If there be any manhood within a man, missing the birth of your first born will do something to you. I would be forever changed. I requested a meeting with the District Attorney and told her I would plead guilty to every charge against Jill. I also proposed they drop all charges on Jill. Thank God they agreed! Again, I returned to the presence of Judge Benefield for the fifth time in my life. This time she sentenced me to four more years. I ACTUALLY FELT SO GOOD! For the first time in my life I did something for someone other than myself; something for my family. That is my definition of manhood!

I was high on meth when I was arrested. I have never used methamphetamine since. Two weeks after my arrest, my son was born and I could proudly say I was no longer a drug user! I did a

Bobby Shane Brooks

total of twenty months in prison then paroled out to my dad's house in Stockbridge, Georgia. Upon my release, I began a job cleaning carpets for a company in Atlanta. I was out only two months before I proposed to Jill. She said yes. What was so cool about Jill is that she didn't wait on me to get out. She went to school and when I was released in March 2005 she was two years away from getting her degree as a Registered Nurse, which she received in 2007. She was determined to turn her life around no matter what decisions I made once I became a free man. I lived at my dad's house for twenty months and incorporated a carpet cleaning company which I called Shane Steamers. I returned to school with the Institute of Inspection Cleaning and Restoration Certification. I am now a Master Textile Cleaner and Master Fire and Smoke Restorer. There are only about fifty people in the state of Georgia with the level of education that I have.

I rented a house and brought Jill and Levi to McDonough to live with me. On November 22, 2007, which just so happened to be Thanksgiving Day, Jill gave birth to our second child. Her name is

Bobby Shane Brooks

Sarah McKayla Brooks. So, I have one child named Levi (which represents the law), and another named Sarah (which represents grace). Can you see where this is going? I bought my first home in September 2008 and Jill and I were married **two years later**.

In December 2011, my spiritual father, Dr. Creflo Dollar began to teach a new revelation on grace. When I first heard "The Grace Message" in 2012, it changed the direction of my life forever. I will tell you in the next chapter how I discovered my real identity.

Bobby Shane Brooks

CHAPTER 6

MINISTRY

As I begin this final chapter my prayer is that through your reading, God has ministered the importance of not only being born again but knowing who you are through the new birth experience. I want you to know that your positive identification and revelation of who you are in Christ is not possible without a constant, daily commitment to renewing your mind. Getting saved happened the moment you accepted Jesus as your personal Lord and Savior (born again). Renewing of the mind is a lifetime process. The reason for that is that your mind, will and emotions do not get born again; only the real you (your spirit) does. Let me explain. Just like God you are a three-part being. As God exists in three parts, the Father, the Son and the Holy Ghost, so you too exist in three parts. You are a spirit, you possess a soul and you live in a physical body. When you have the born again experience your spirit is not regenerated by God. NO! He recreated it! God actually replaces the old spirit, born in the likeness of Adam, with the spirit born in the likeness of God. Your mind, will and emotions (your soul) or as I prefer to call them; the thinker, the feeler and the chooser, do not get replaced. You also have the exact same body you had prior to being born again. Now you have a new spirit that completely agrees with God's Word. Your soul, however must be retrained through a daily renewing process to bring it into agreement with the new recreated spirit; "the REAL you". As you initiate the process of renewing the mind daily through the Word, your soul will begin to agree more and more with the "New Man". Following this, you will bring your physical body (or the flesh) into submission to the new righteous, holy, redeemed identity. On its own, your body will never agree with the Word of God. In fact the residue from the old man will always try to persuade you to act according to the desires of the flesh and to extract your identity from that old behavior....YOU MUST NOT DO THAT! As you have read these previous chapters it is plain to see that this is exactly what happened to me. I was born again without a renewed mind and my life was characterized by my old behavior of acting like a heathen. If you believe right, then you will live right. Let me

Bobby Shane Brooks

show you some great scriptures that define your true positive identification. These scriptures will help you begin to act like who you really are. If you are born again, you are a Child of the King!

Anytime Satan speaks, he does so with a string attached to your identity. When you are born again you are actually someone he can never be. You are recreated in the likeness of God and that is something he desperately wants, but will never have! Satan tries to get you to think and talk like him and that does not line up with your true identity. The devil has no hope, therefore he tries to get you to believe you have no hope. He is the absolute definition of depression so he tries to persuade you into a state of depression. Satan tries to persuade you to choose a false identity based on behavior, feelings, or anything other than the Word. But the Word is exactly where we Christians get our true identity! I am telling you, knowing who you are in Christ is the key to the entire Christian walk. This enforces the total defeat of Satan Jesus has already taken care of for us. Genesis 1:26-27 says, "*And God said, Let us make man in our image, after our likeness: and let them have dominion* over the fish *of the sea, and over the fowl of the air, and over the cattle, and over all the*

Bobby Shane Brooks

earth, and over every creeping thing that creepeth upon the earth. So God created man in his own image, in the image of God created he him; male and female created he them". So it is plain to see that God made man in His own image. I believe you can safely say they were speaking spirits just like God. What I am about to share with you is the first known case of identity theft. Genesis 3:1-5 says, *"Now the serpent was more subtil than any beast of the field which the Lord God had made. And he said unto the woman, Yea, hath God said, Ye shall not eat of every tree of the garden? And the woman said unto the serpent, We may eat of the fruit of the trees of the garden: But of the fruit of the tree which is in the midst of the garden, God hath said, Ye shall not eat of it, neither shall ye touch it, lest ye die. And the serpent said unto the woman, Ye shall not surely die: For God doth know that in the day ye eat thereof, then your eyes shall be opened, and ye shall be as gods, knowing good and evil. "* Satan told her she had to do something in order to become something that both she and Adam already were! They were already created in God's image and they already were like gods! Satan even tried the same trick with Jesus, but I am so glad that our Savior knew who He was!

Bobby Shane Brooks

Let's look at Matthew 3:17 - 4:3. The scripture says, *"And lo a voice from heaven, saying, This is my beloved Son, in whom I am well pleased. Then was Jesus led up of the Spirit into the wilderness to be tempted of the devil. And when he had fasted forty days and forty nights, he was afterward hungred. And when the tempter came to him, he said, If thou be the Son of God, command that these stones be made bread."* God called Jesus His "beloved" Son; Satan said "if thou be the Son..." What happened to the beloved part? Satan tried to get Jesus to question His very own identity, but Jesus didn't fall for it like Adam and Eve had. It is of utmost importance to know who you are! According to John 10:10 Satan is primarily a thief and stealing your God given ID is his prerogative. His mission is to convince you that you are not who God and His Word says you are.

Let's look at 2 Corinthians 5:17-21, *"Therefore if any man be in Christ, he is a new creature: old things are passed away; behold, all things are become new. And all things are of God, who hath reconciled us to himself by Jesus Christ, and hath given to us the ministry of reconciliation; To wit, that God was in Christ, reconciling the world unto himself, not imputing their trespasses*

Bobby Shane Brooks

unto them; and hath committed unto us the word of reconciliation. Now then we are ambassadors for Christ, as though God did beseech you by us: we pray you in Christ's stead, be ye reconciled to God. For he hath made him to be sin for us, who knew no sin; that we might be made the righteousness of God in him." You get that? He was made sin. You were made righteous! The most marvelous thing that has ever happened! God is reconciling ungodly men unto Himself and declaring those men righteous. That is Gospel. News that sounds almost too good to be true, but it is. To say that you are not righteous because of your behavior, after God says you are, because of Jesus obedience, is saying the Blood of Jesus isn't sufficient. If you believe you are the righteousness of God, your behavior will begin to line up with that God given identity. Check out the Mirror Bible translation, *"Now, in the light of your co-inclusion in his death and resurrection, whoever you thought you were before, in Christ you are a brand new person! The old ways of seeing yourself and everyone else are over. Acquaint yourself with the new! (Just imagine this!) Whoever a person was as a Jew, Greek, slave or freeman, Boer, Zulu, Xhosa, British, Indian, Muslim or*

Bobby Shane Brooks

American, Chinese, Japanese or Congolese; is now dead and gone!
They all died when Jesus died! Remember we are not talking law
language here! The 'If' in, "If any man is in Christ" is not a
condition, it is the conclusion of the revelation of the gospel! Man is
in Christ by God's doing [1 Corinthians 1:30 and Ephesians 1:4].
The verses of 2 Corinthians 5:14-16 give context to verse 17! For so
long we studied verse 17 on its own and interpreted the 'if' as a
condition! Paul did not say, "If any man is in Christ," he said
"THEREFORE if any man is in Christ ..." The "therefore"
immediately includes verses 14 to 16! If God's faith sees every man
in Christ in his death, then they were certainly also in Christ in his
resurrection. Jesus did not reveal a "potential" you, he revealed the
truth about you so that you may know the truth about yourself and be
free indeed! In the death and resurrection of Jesus Christ, God did
not redeem a compromised replica of you; he rescued the original,
blueprint you, created in his radiant mirror likeness! Any other 'self'
you're trying to find or esteem will disappoint! Reckon your 'DIY-
law of works-self' dead, and your redeemed self co-raised and co-
seated together with Christ! This is freedom indeed! Galatians 2:19-

Bobby Shane Brooks

20; Romans 6:11 and

1 Peter 1:3. We are reconnected with our original genesis through the resurrection of Jesus from the dead! This new birth endorses and celebrates the hope of the ages; God's eternal love dream concludes in life!) To now see everything as new is to simply see what God has always known in Christ; we are not debating man's experience, opinion, or his contribution; this is 100% God's belief and his doing. In Jesus Christ, God exchanged equivalent value to redeem us to himself. This act of reconciliation is the mandate of our ministry. (The word, katalasso, translates as reconciliation; a mutual exchange of equal value.) Our ministry declares that Jesus did not act independently of God. Christ is proof that God reconciled the total kosmos to himself. Deity and humanity embraced in Christ; the fallen state of mankind was deleted; their trespasses would no longer count against them! God has placed this message in us. He now announces his friendship with every individual from within us! (God was in Christ, when he reconciled the world to himself. The incarnation did not separate the Father from the Son and the Spirit. In him dwells the fullness of God in a human body (Colossians 2:9).

Bobby Shane Brooks

As a man, Jesus felt the agony of fallen humanity on the cross when he echoed in Psalm 22, "My God, my God, why have you forsaken me! Why are you so far from helping me, from the words of my groaning?" But then in verse 24, he declares: "He has not despised or abhorred the affliction of the afflicted; and he has not hid his face from him, but has heard, when he cried to him." The voice God has in Christ he now has in us; we are God's ambassadors. Our lives exhibit the urgency of God to persuade everyone to realize the reconciliation of their redeemed identity.

- *The word, parakaleo, comes from para, a preposition indicating close proximity, a thing proceeding from a sphere of influence, with a suggestion of union of place of residence, to have sprung from its author and giver, originating from, denoting the point from which an action originates, intimate connection, and kaleo, to identify by name, to surname.*

In Luke 15:28, 31, his father pleaded with him, "My child, you are always with me, and all that I have is yours." "Be reconciled" could not be translated, "Become reconciled!" "Do in order to become" is the language of the Old Testament; the language of the New Testament is, "Be, because of what was done!" This is the divine exchange: he who knew no sin embraced our

Bobby Shane Brooks

distortion; he appeared to be without form; this was the mystery of God's prophetic poetry. He was disguised in our distorted image, marred with our iniquities; he took our sorrows, our pain, our shame to his grave and birthed his righteousness in us. He took our sins and we became his innocence. (The word, hamartia, comes from ha, without, and meros, form. The word, poema, often translated "made" like in, "he was made to be sin." However, because of its context here I have translated poema to read prophetic poetry. As the scapegoat of the human race, he took on the distorted image of fallen man, he did not become a sinner, but the official representative of humanity's sin. Then Paul uses the word ginomai, he birthed his righteousness in us; since we were born anew in his resurrection from the dead. Hosea 6:2, Ephesian 2:5, 1 Pet 1:3.

In Isaiah 52:10 it says, "The Lord has bared his holy arm before the eyes of all the nations, and all the ends of the earth shall see the salvation of our God. Isaiah 52:14-15 says, "Just as many were astonished at you—so was he marred in his appearance, more than any human - and his form beyond that of human semblance—so

Bobby Shane Brooks

will he startle many nations. Kings will shut their mouths because of him; for what had not been told them they will see, and what they had not heard they will understand. Isaiah 53:4-5 Surely, he has borne our griefs, and carried our sorrows; yet we esteemed him stricken, smitten of God, and afflicted. But he was wounded by our transgressions; he was bruised by our iniquities; the chastisement of our peace was on him; and with his stripes we ourselves are healed (RSV). He was not bruised by God but by the very humanity he was about to redeem! Neither was he bruised for our iniquities, but by our iniquities! Greek dia, because of; by. Sadly Isaiah 53:10 is translated, "It pleased the Lord to bruise him!" We have seen that the whole passage says again and again that it was men who killed the Servant and crushed him. The Greek Septuagint of this verse, written 200 years before Christ, by Jewish Hebrew scholars who were fluent in their native tongue and Greek and had access to even more ancient original manuscripts, have rendered the Hebrew text as follows: when the Greek text is translated into English it says: "and the Lord desires to purify him [the Servant] of the plague!" The original Hebrew language is untranslatable! Look at what

Bobby Shane Brooks

translators of the New Revised Standard Version say on their footnotes to this verse: "meaning of Hebrew uncertain." Koine Greek was the lingua franca of Alexandria, Egypt and the Eastern Mediterranean at the time. The Septuagint was in regular use in New Testament times and often quoted, particularly in the Pauline epistles, and also by the Apostolic Fathers and later Greek Church Fathers.

Deuteronomy 32:5-6, "They have corrupted themselves; they did not behave as his children, they have become a distorted generation of people, twisted out of their true pattern; they are a crooked and perverse generation". (Paul also quotes this verse in Philippians 2:15.) Deuteronomy 32:18. "You were unmindful of the Rock that begot you, and you forgot the God who gave you birth".

Romans 8:29, " He pre-designed and engineered us from the start to be jointly fashioned in the same mold and image of his son according to the exact blueprint of his thought". We see the original and intended pattern of our lives preserved in his Son. He is the firstborn from the same womb that reveals our genesis. He confirms that we are the invention of God. (We were born anew when he was

Bobby Shane Brooks

raised from the dead [1 Peter 1:3]! His resurrection co-reveals our common genesis as well as our redeemed innocence. [Roman 4:25 and Acts 17:31] No wonder then that he is not ashamed to call us his brethren! We indeed share the same origin [Hebrews 2:11], and, "In him we live and move and have our being. We are indeed his offspring!" [Acts 17:28]. In Romans 8:30 Jesus reveals that man pre-existed in God; he defines us. He justified us and also glorified us. He redeemed our innocence and restored the glory we lost in Adam. [Romans 3:23, 24: the word, prohoritso, means pre defined, like when an architect draws up a detailed plan; and the word, kaleo, to surname, identify by name.]

[II Corinthians 5:17-21]: The Mirror. Wow, what a mouthful of truth!

Some people believe that we are born in Gods image but we are not. All humans are born in Adams image. Genesis 5:13 says, *"This is the book of the generations of Adam. In the day that God created man, in the likeness of God made he him; Male and female created he them; and blessed them, and called their name Adam, in the day when they were created. And Adam lived an hundred and thirty years, and begat a son in his own likeness, after his image;*

and called his name Seth:" So Adam was created in Gods image.

Then the fall took place and Adam gave away his true ID. When he

had Seth, his own son took on the image of fallen Adam. Seth did

not have Gods image! Satan is the original perpetrator of ID theft.

Because of the fall we are born in Adams image, not Gods. We must

be born again to regain our original God intended ID. Colossians

3:9, "Lie not one to another, seeing that ye have put off the old man

with his deeds;" You put off the old man! This is how The Mirror

translates the same scripture, "That old life was a lie, foreign to our

design! Those garments of disguise are now thoroughly stripped off

us in our understanding of our union with Christ in his death and

resurrection. We are no longer obliged to live under the identity and

rule of the robes we wore before; neither are we cheating anyone

through false pretensions. The garments an actor would wear define

his part in the play but cannot define him [Colossians 3:9].

This thing is starting to make perfect sense, right? Ephesians

4:20-24, ""*But ye have not so learned Christ; If so be that ye have*

heard him, and have been taught by him, as the truth is in Jesus:

Bobby Shane Brooks

That ye put off concerning the former conversation the old man, which is corrupt according to the deceitful lusts; And be renewed in the spirit of your mind; And that ye put on the new man, which after God is created in righteousness and true holiness." The translator of The Mirror puts it this way, "Of what total contrast is Christ! It is not possible to study Christ in any other context; he is the incarnation, hear him resonate within you! The truth about you has its ultimate reference in Jesus. ("The truth as it is in Christ." He did not come to introduce a new compromised set of rules; he is not an example for us but of us!) Now you are free to strip off that old identity like a filthy worn-out garment. Lust corrupted you and cheated you into wearing it. (Just like an actor who wore a cloak for a specific role he had to interpret; the fake identity is no longer appropriate!) Be renewed in your innermost mind. (Ponder the truth about you, as it is displayed in Christ; begin with the fact of your co-seatedness.) This will cause you to be completely reprogrammed in the way you think about yourself! Notice that Paul does not say, "Renew your minds!" This transformation happens in the spirit of your mind, awakened by truth on a much deeper level than a mere intellectual or academic

Bobby Shane Brooks

consent. We often thought we had to get information to drop from the head to the heart; but it is the other way around! Jesus says in John 7:38, "*When you believe that I am what the scriptures are all about, then you will discover that you are what I am all about, and rivers of living waters will gush out of your innermost being!*". The spirit of man was never contaminated; just like the watermark in a paper note. The lost coin never lost its original inscription and image [see also James 3:9]; it was the mind that was veiled by darkness; we were darkened in our understanding! Our thoughts were reduced to the soul realm reference, knowing ourselves, and one another merely after the flesh. Isiah 55:8-11 "There is nothing wrong with our design or our redemption; we were thinking wrong! In order for our thoughts to be rescued from the dominion of darkness, Jesus as the incarnate image and likeness of God, has gone into our darkest hellish nightmare, and faced our cruelest judgment and fears, and died our death! This is the mystery that was hidden for ages and generations, for our glorification! We were co-crucified, to bring absolute closure to every reference we have had of ourselves as a result of Adam's fall! And while we were dead in our sins and trespasses, God co-quickened us and co-raised us, and co-seated us in Christ! Now, we all with unveiled faces may behold the glory of the Lord as in a mirror! And be radically transformed in our thinking in order to rediscover his image and likeness fully redeemed in us!) Immerse yourself into this God-shaped new man from above! You are created in the image and likeness of God. This is what righteousness and true holiness are all about." Mr. Francis du Toit nailed it when he translated this marvelous scripture.

Religion has always fought Christians to convince us we are not like Jesus, but the Word tells us that if we are in covenant relationship with Jesus we are just like Him! 1 John 4:7 and 17 reads, *"Beloved, let us love one another: for love is of God; and every one that loveth is born of God, and knoweth God.*

Herein is our love made perfect, that we may have boldness in the day of judgment: because as he is, so are we in this world." So I ask you is Jesus sick? NO! Is Jesus broke? NO! Is Jesus in bondage or experiencing any form of addiction? Emphatically NO!! Then we ,as believers, are not any of those things either. We are as blameless in this life as Jesus is no matter the contradiction in the flesh. Our

Bobby Shane Brooks

flesh does not tell us who we are. The world does not dictate who we are. Jehovah Himself tells us who we are! Say it with me, "I am the righteousness of God by faith in Christ Jesus!" Your spirit is heaven ready now, there will not be a final polish to get us ready. We are born again and ready now! If Satan can get us to agree with him that we are not like Jesus we will believe a false identity. 1 Corinthians 6:17 says, *"But he that is joined unto the Lord is one spirit."* Are you joined unto the Lord? If you are born again you are, so don't allow anyone to teach you that when you sin or miss the mark that you have fallen out of "fellowship" with Jesus. That is a lie. Who do you think will counsel you out of a ditch when you fall into it? He has such an investment in you! According to the writer of Hebrews He will never leave you or forsake you. The word *never* means just that, NEVER. It is an accounting term and the same word is used in Romans when Paul says that the Lord will not impute sin on your account. To do so would be the same as saying the blood of Jesus is not all sufficient when in fact the blood of Jesus is actually more than enough!

Bobby Shane Brooks

I am going to end this book by proving you have not only been made righteous (you did not become righteous you were made righteous), and not only have you been redeemed and bought back with the currency of Jesus own blood but you are HOLY! People have a hard time believing this because they are listening to their flesh and aren't inclined to what God says about them regardless of behavior. Remember it is not based on your behavior but on Jesus' obedience! Let's look at 1 Corinthians 1:20-30. The Word says, *"That no flesh should glory in his presence. But of him are ye in Christ Jesus, who of God is made unto us wisdom, and righteousness, and sanctification, and redemption:"* Guess what the Greek word for sanctification is? That's right HOLINESS! Jesus is your holiness. You are holy because of the finished work of Jesus. If you say that you are not holy you are really saying Jesus is not holy and we all know Jesus defines holiness. Check out the Amplified version, *"So that no mortal man should [have pretense for glorying and] boast in the presence of God. But it is from Him that you have your life in Christ Jesus, Whom God made our Wisdom from God, [revealed to us a knowledge of the divine plan of salvation*

Bobby Shane Brooks

previously hidden, manifesting itself as] our Righteousness [thus making us upright and putting us in right standing with God], and our Consecration [making us pure and holy], and our Redemption [providing our ransom from eternal penalty for sin]." You are in right standing with God not because of anything that you've done but only because of what Jesus did. The Mirror reads, "Of God's doing are we in Christ. He is both the genesis and genius of our wisdom; a wisdom that reveals how righteous, sanctified and redeemed we are in Him. (The preposition, ek, always denotes origin, source. Mankind's association in Christ is God's doing. In God's economy, Christ represents us. God's faith accomplished in Christ what man could never achieve through personal discipline and willpower as taught in every religion. Of His design we are in Christ; we are associated in oneness with Him. Our wisdom is sourced in this union! Also, our righteousness and holiness originate from Him. Holiness equals wholeness and harmony of man's spirit, soul, and body. Our redemption is sanctioned in Him. He redeemed our identity, sanity, health, joy, peace, innocence, and complete well-being [See Ephesians 1:4]! The Knox Translation reads, "It is from

Bobby Shane Brooks

him that we take our origin.") He is our claim to fame. (This is what Jeremiah meant when he wrote: "Let not the wise man glory in his wisdom, let not the mighty man glory in his might, let not the rich man glory in his riches; but let him who glories glory in this, that he understands and knows me, that I am the Lord who practices steadfast love, justice, and righteousness in the earth; for in these things do I delight, says the Lord." [Jeremiah 9:23, 24 — RSV]) [I Corinthians 1:30-31]

Can I share, what a joy it has been for me to write this book just for you. First and foremost, I want you to receive Jesus as your Savior, then know who you are in Jesus. What a masterpiece you are with worth equivalent to the price He paid Himself with His own body and blood. Let's face it, in reality He loves you so much. I am thankful for the anointing He placed on my life to explain, through the scriptures, what actually takes place when someone experiences the new birth. Reader, I pray that your eyes, ears and mind are opened to the real truth about who God has made you!

Now you are free to strip off that old identity like a filthy worn-out garment. Lust corrupted you and cheated you into wearing

Bobby Shane Brooks

it. (Just like an actor who wore a cloak for a specific role he had to interpret; the fake identity is no longer appropriate!) Be renewed in your innermost mind. (Ponder the truth about you, as it is displayed in Christ; begin with the fact of your co-seatedness.) This will cause you to be completely reprogrammed in the way you think about yourself! Notice that Paul does not say, "Renew your minds!" This transformation happens in the spirit of your mind, awakened by truth on a much deeper level than a mere intellectual or academic consent. We often thought that we had to get information to drop from the head to the heart; but it is the other way around! Jesus says in John 7:38, "When you believe that I am what the scriptures are all about, then you will discover that you are what I am all about, and rivers of living waters will gush out of your innermost being! The spirit of man was never contaminated; just like the watermark in a paper note. The lost coin never lost its original inscription and image [see also James 3:9]; it was the mind that was veiled by darkness; we were darkened in our understanding! Our thoughts were reduced to the soul realm reference, knowing ourselves, and one another merely after the flesh. Isa 55:8-11. There is nothing wrong with our design or our redemption; we were thinking wrong! In order for our thoughts to be rescued from the dominion of darkness, Jesus as the incarnate image and likeness of God, has gone into our darkest hellish nightmare, and faced our cruelest judgment and fears, and died our death! This is the mystery that was hidden for ages and generations, for our glorification! We were co-crucified, to bring absolute closure to every reference we have had of ourselves as a result of Adam's fall! And while we were dead in our sins and trespasses, God co-quickened us and co-raised us, and co-seated us in Christ! Now, we all with unveiled faces may behold the glory of the Lord as in a mirror! And be radically transformed in our thinking in order to rediscover his image and likeness fully redeemed in us!) [Ephesians 4:22-23] *The Mirror Bible.* This wonderful scripture really sums up my purpose for writing this book, so that Christians can begin to comprehend that the "new birth" is definitely more than fire insurance but through the experience we are given our real identities!

Bobby Shane Brooks

God has identified us. Who can disqualify us? His Word is our origin. No one can point a finger; He declared us innocent. The word kaleo, means to identify by name, to surname. The word eklektos suggests that we have our origin in God's thought; from ek, source, and lego, to communicate. He has placed us beyond the reach of blame, shame, guilt and gossip!

Romans 8:33, *"Who shall bring any charge against God's elect [when it is] God Who justifies [that is, Who puts us in right relation to Himself? Who shall come forward and accuse or impeach those whom God has chosen? Will God, Who acquits us?]"*

Bobby Shane Brooks

CALL TO SALVATION

Romans 10:9-10 (Amplified) states, *"Because if you acknowledge and confess with your lips that Jesus is Lord and in your heart believe (adhere to, trust in, and rely on the truth) that God raised Him from the dead, you will be saved. For with the heart a person believes (adheres to, trusts in, and relies on Christ) and so is justified (declared righteous, acceptable to Christ), and with the mouth he confesses (declares openly and speaks out freely his faith) and confirms his salvation"*.

After reading this book, if you are ready to accept your new identity and become a born again believer please repeat after me: *I, (state your name) know that Jesus is Lord and I believe that God raised Him from the dead.* You are now saved! Wasn't that easy? Now study and renew your mind with the Word of God so that you can walk in your rue identity, and claim all the things that God has for you. He loves you and so do I.

Bobby Shane Brooks

About the Author

Bobby Shane Brooks is a husband and father of two. Born and raised in Atlanta, Georgia, Shane owns a carpet cleaning business; Shane Steamers, and is a full time student at World Changers Bible School, Class of 2017.

Made in the USA
Columbia, SC
18 July 2019